AL S

Music's Divine
New Divas

An unauthorized biography
by Sheryl Altman

A Division of HarperCollins*Publishers*

ACKNOWLEDGMENTS

*Thanks to: my first partner in print, Holly Gates Russell, for
giving me wings; to my little sis Deb, for inspiring my interest in
The British Invasion: and to Nancy and Pete's new angel, Emily
Mae Saperstone—don't worry, she'll be into All Saints in no time!*
—Sheryl

ISBN: 0-06-107146-3
Library of Congress catalog card number: 98-72309
1 2 3 4 5 6 7 8 9 10
❖
First Edition, 1998

Visit us on the World Wide Web!
http://www.harperchildrens.com

To my husband, (Saint) Peter:
Life with you is heavenly . . .

Dear Fellow Fans:

Okay . . . I'm no saint.

I admit to calling in sick sometimes when I'm not, and telling my best friend her new hairdo looks awesome when even a mohawk would be more attractive.

I have politely passed on many a Mr. Wrong with a little white lie: "Sorry, my pet goldfish is having a health crisis. I just can't leave him alone Saturday night."

But even with all my indiscretions I like to think of myself as a strong candidate for All Sainthood.

My posse of gal pals—Noreen, Stacy, Pam, and Holly—will snicker when they read this: "Miss Do-Everything-by-the-*Book* is a bad girl? Oh, Pull-lease!"

So you won't catch me wearing snowboard gear and Doc Martens to my office, or tattooing a dragon my derriere. I can still belt out "Bootie Call" with the best of them. I make a mean cup of English Breakfast tea. And I bought an Adidas running suit in neon purple so I can look fresh, fly, and funky (and oh-so-Shaz) jogging through Central Park.

Besides, All Saints isn't about how you dress. It isn't even just the hottest girl group to hit the CD racks recently. It's an attitude: confidence, coolness, and charisma. It's four women—Shaz, Nic, Mel, and Nat—not just with some catchy motto but a mission: Be bold! Be brave! Be baaaaaad! And above all else, be yourself.

All Saints is where it's at, and where you'll find me. Shhh! It'll be our little secret. . . .

—Sheryl

Contents

Chapter 1
The Saints Come Marching In

*Y*ou could call them the Fab Four but *that* name is already taken. Meet Nic, Nat, Mel, and Shaz—the All Saints.

Still looking to label them? Try All Sexy. All Sassy. All Music. Spice is nice, but All Saints are "All That and More!"

They groove. They move. And like their hit single says, they "Know Where It's At." Maybe that's why millions of fans worldwide are keen to copy their clothes, their coifs, and their coy come-hither stares. Their music speaks to everyone: it's sensual and strong—what every woman wants to be. So how could you not be hooked?

How'd it all start? Let Shaznay Lewis spin the tale:

"We worked our bums off, perfecting an original sound," she told a source.

In the early '90s she and Melanie Blatt, still teens, were hanging out at a studio on funky All Saints Road in West London. They were just making tea and laying down backgrounds in exchange for some studio time to record their own tracks. They put out a single ("Silver Shadow") with another girl— Simone Rainford—but it didn't do as well as they had hoped. Then they signed briefly with ZTT Records, where they released a second single, "If You Wanna Party." Sadly, that deal fell flat, too.

"We didn't know what direction we wanted to go in," says Mel. "And ZTT didn't really know what to do with us, so it was a pretty short-lived thing."

"We did a lot of things we didn't believe in, because we were told it was the right thing to do," says Shaz. "But at the end of the day, it's about the music."

So it was back to the drawing board. In 1995, just when the proto-Saints thought they had a few tunes that were record-ready, Mel bumped into some old mates from school, Natalie and Nicole Appleton (she had known them since she was eleven), and impulsively asked them to join up. Their four voices meshed together in heavenly harmony, and they released their first single, "I Know Where It's At," on the London Records label in August 1997 in the U.K., and January 1998 in the U.S. Their self-titled album hit U.K. stores in November 1997, and here in the States in March 1998.

London's chairman, Tracy Bennett, was wowed the minute he heard their demo: "This is a marriage—it's going to last. All Saints are going to be the biggest band in the world," he says.

And he should know. In the past twenty years he's signed Fine Young Cannibals, East 17, and Bananarama. Now, with their manager, John Benson, the record company's enthusiasm, and a stable of awesome producers, they've hit their stride with pride.

Who's on board? Cameron McVey, who worked with Massive Attack and Neneh Cherry; Nellee Hooper, who molded Madonna's, Björk's, and Janet Jackson's tracks; and Johnny Douglas, of George Michael's team. Magnus Fiennes (yes, *Avengers* star Ralph is his big brother) co-produced the project.

In a few weeks All Saints' first single climbed the Brit charts to number four. Their second single, "Never Ever," hit number one in Great Britain and Australia, went quadruple-platinum (so far!), and won two British Music Awards this year, for best single and video. Closer to home, their first U.S. release, "I Know Where It's At," is aiming for the top of Billboard's Heat Seekers chart. Their third release, a double A side of "Under the Bridge" and "Lady Marmalade," hit the stores on April 20th—and was an instant sellout. Want more? Try Top 10 in Japan and Holland . . .

With that kind of success, you know comparisons are inevitable. Spice Girls, the hottest British export of the 1990s, ruled radio stations and record sales. They boasted a movie, major commercial endorsements for Pepsi, and a twelve-minute sellout at Madison Square Garden for their upcoming NYC concert in summer 1998. "Who will step up to try and claim their throne?" the tabloids ask. Enter All Saints.

When the British rags declared war, All Saints—striving to make a name for themselves—bristled at being dubbed Spice clones.

"Respect to the Spice Girls for what they're doing," Shaz told *Smash Hits*. "They make a lot of people happy . . . being compared to them is not a bad thing exactly. But if people are still going on about it a year from now, then we'll be angry. Our music's different. For their part, the Spice Girls have dismissed rumors of a falling-out with All Saints, as they prepared to kick off their world tour—by raving about their rivals' album. They even say the Saints CD will be a fave on the tour bus. How's that for Girl Power?

All Saints write all of their own material and their sound is much more soul, R&B, and hip-hop than Spice. They insist that instant

fame is not what they're after. Want proof?
Rumor has it they turned down a Pepsi
campaign and refused to choose a slogan (à
la Spice Girls' "Girl Power").

"Money isn't everything. If that was what
we wanted, we would have done it years
ago," says Shaz. The band had been plugging
away trying to perfect their sound, and turned
down numerous record deals until they were
ready.

Before London Records came along, Sony
and others were anxious to sign the girls and
strike lightning twice with a new Spice.
Luckily, the ladies held out. "Who wants to be
told how to look and what to say?" says Mel.
"We're not pushovers. People see four young
girls and they think they can manipulate us.
The only thing that matters to us is our music.
We're about being as honest as possible—All
Saints is all us—no fabricated, formulated
image."

Keepin' it real is their goal. "We never
thought, 'We want to be this' or 'We want
to be that,'" Nic told *React* magazine.
"We've just done what comes naturally to

us, and so far, it's working."

Some advice to the competition? Better say your prayers!

Where Can You Catch Them?

- For starters, on *Saturday Night Live* (they performed with their guest band April 11, 1998)
- in movie theaters in a nine-minute trailer before *Jackie Brown*
- zipping off to another zip code: if negotiations work out, they'll guest on *Beverly Hills, 90210*
- they've also appeared on *Regis & Kathie Lee*
- they've promised to embark on a world tour by the beginning of 1999

Saint Nice to Spread Rumors!

Rate the tabloid tales "fact" or "fiction" and check your score below:

1. The All Saints are making a movie co-starring Robert De Niro.

2. Nic and Nat once battled over the same boy.

3. Baby Spice beat up Nicky when they were schoolmates.

4. The Saints fired their first manager.

ANSWERS:

1. Fiction. This tab story came from a joke Mel made. No "Saintsworld" is in the works yet!

2. Fact. "We once dated the same guy, but then we decided he wasn't worth it," says Nat.

3. Fiction. Baby Spice and Nicky were friendly in school.

4. Fact. The girls gave Paul Hallett his walking papers just before signing to London's label.

Are You a Saint or a Sinner?

1. That hot guy in homeroom asked you out for Friday night. You already said you'd hang with your gal pals. You:

(a) blow off your buds — Studmuffin comes first!

(b) reschedule with Romeo

2. Your little sis is sweating over an English lit midterm. You:

    (a) suggest she invest in Cliff's Notes

    (b) help her cram for the exam

3. You score a totally hot slipdress at the mall, but Mom says it's too trashy. You:

    (a) keep it anyway—she'll never look in the back of your closet

    (b) return it—Mom knows best

4. Your 'rents insist on meeting the new guy. Did you forget to mention he's got a tattoo the size of Cleveland on his arm? You:

    (a) lie—tell them he's history

    (b) ask him to stop by for milk and cookies

5. Your idea of an awesome ensemble is:

    (a) a teeny tank with tight jeans

    (b) a silk blouse and flowery floor-length skirt

HOW YOU RATE:

Mostly A's—you little devil, you!

Mostly B's—you make the Church Lady look naughty.

A mix of A's and B's—you're more Saintly than you think!

Chapter 2
Their Hood

*W*here does that Saintly coolness come from? It's all in the accent!

The girls will be the first to tell you that their home turf, England, is on the cutting edge of fashion, food, and fun—not to mention music. What are the hot clubs and hubs where you might find the foursome? Here's the lowdown on London town (pack your passports!). If you can't catch a flight soon, drop some of these sites into your conversation—your friends will think you're way well traveled.

Rooms with a View

Every celeb from RuPaul to Sting to Snoop Doggy Dogg heads to the Halcyon Hotel. Isn't that Puff Daddy dining under a desert tent in The Egyptian Room?

Stars seeking to slum—like Madonna and Michael Jackson—check into Columbia. Okay, it's a dive, but rock 'n' rollers find it the perfect hideaway (who would believe that a star stays here?).

The Lanesborough provides all the extras: fax machine, umbrella, and infrared security system ready in your room. It'll cost big bucks, but you can also have a butler of your very own.

Young Hollywood, supermodels, and the music biz make a beeline to Metropolitan. Its Met Bar is the hangout du jour, always packed to capacity with pretty young things sipping martinis.

Can't afford the four-figure tab for a visit to any of the above? The Holland House Youth Hostel is happening. Not just your average dorm, it's built on the remains of an old mansion. And there's always Old Reliable: Holiday Inn.

Clubland

The Brits have their own brand of beats. When they're looking for inspiration (or to shake some bootie) the All Saints might head to these hot spots.

Brixton Academy: A huge loftlike hall in South London along the lines of NYC's Webster Hall. *Time Out* mag likes to list its events (practically every night there's a different theme, e.g., "Reggae Renegade Party"). Frequently showcases up-and-coming alternative acts.

Annabel's: Forget getting in unless you know someone ("But really—I'm the fifth All Saint!"). This place makes penetrating LA's exclusive Viper Room and Roxy look like a breeze. It's members-only and snobs abound. Hey, isn't that you-know-who hangin' at the bar?

Mwah Mwah: The name of this club is the sound a double air-kiss makes (cute, huh?). A fave underage hangout in Chelsea. Its big-sister club is Beach Blanket Bingo, a gothic dance hall in Portobello à la NYC's Limelight.

Both rock, and rule, on the weekends.

Jazz Café: Not just a jazz joint, this converted bank in downtown Camden has spotlighted everyone from Echo & the Bunnymen and Debbie Harry to Boy George and Massive Attack. Similar to NYC's Bottom Line, it's a fun spot for acts to try out new material.

Live and On-Person!

THE place to play in England is Wembley Stadium. It's mega—like Madison Square Garden or Nassau Coliseum—and has hosted the likes of Madonna and U2. Apollo, Shepherds Bush Empire, and the Royal Albert Hall are smaller but just as star-packed. Eric Clapton traditionally plays ten days at The Hall in February.

Radio Stations

What waves will you want to tune to when in England? 1FM–98.8 FM, Capitol FM, Virgin–105.8 FM, and Kiss FM all spin the Saints' sound.

England Eats

Tootsies is where the Saints score crinkle-cut fries and greasy burgers (just like in the States!).

Chicago Pizza Pie Factory serves up slices with the works.

The Ivy or The Savoy is where you'll find superstars supping.

Shop Till You Drop

Underwear is an obsession with All Saints. The girls go to M&S (Marks & Spencer) on Oxford Street for unmentionables ("Avoid the granny department," advises Nat). Other Brit boutiques: Agent Provocateur for funky tangerine fishnet stockings and Skin Two for spandex.

Shaz satisfies a sweet tooth ("If there's an Oreo cookie in a jar she'll eat it," swears Nic) at Rococo, a chocoholics' haven on King's Road.

Hyperhip club kids go to Red or Dead, Top Shop, Trax, and Jigsaw, or hang at Kensington Market (England's answer to the mall) on the weekend.

The haute couture crowd buys at Prada, Vivienne Westwood, Versace, and Katharine Hamnett.

Where can you suit up like a Saint in Air Maxx or Adidas? Lillywhite's is a jock's best friend.

The Tourist Traps

You'll want to scope out all the sites, including Westminster Abbey, Big Ben, Buckingham Palace, and Trafalgar Square while you're there. But those in the know prefer the neighborhood haunts: Portobello Road, Camden Lock, and King's Cross. Of course the rad restaurants and stores on All Saints Road (our fave group's namesake) are a prerequisite!

Going on Holiday?

Pick what you'd drag in your bag on a trip to the U.K. Then check your choices below to see what the items you can't leave home without reveal about you:

1. makeup bag stuffed to capacity
2. scissors

3. map of the sites
4. sunscreen
5. an All Saints baseball cap
6. camera
7. teeny-weeny polka-dot bikini
8. umbrella
9. Band-Aids
10. your cell phone
11. flashlight

How You See Yourself

Makeup: You love to snag the spotlight with a drama queen visage.

Bikini: You've got it and you love to flaunt it.

Camera: You're a bit sentimental—bring some tissues on your trip, too.

How Others See You

Band-Aids: You're practical and able to solve problems.

Umbrella: You're a loyal bud who'll always be there when friends call.

Sunscreen: You're protective of your pals.

What's Your Destiny?

Scissors: You've got a big decision to make soon—will you cut some ties that bind?

Map: You like to have a plan—but try to be a little spontaneous in the next few months.

Flashlight: You tend to look on the bright side. This will get you through a sticky situation in the next few months.

Way-cool Web Sites About the Brits

http://www.a-london-guide.co.uk

http://www.ps2.com/pkp/city/travel/england.htm

http://www.vacations.com/Vacations/Europe/Great-britain/Editorial/London/tips.html

http://www.rdn.de/ce/lon/LONTips.html
Cool clubs and who's in concert

For more info on The Saints' scenes, check out these books:

Frommer's Irreverent Guide to London

Frommer's London by Night

London Lingo

Gear up, Guv'ner, to speak like a bloomin' Brit:

Blimey! (exclamation): Like "Ohmigod!"

Bloke (noun): A guy. Nic was way popular with the blokes in high school.

Bloody (adverb): Very, extremely. Nat described the streets of New York as "bloody crowded."

Dosh (noun): Bucks, cash, dinero, moola. "I spend lots of dosh on makeup," fesses Nat.

Fancy (verb): Like, want, desire, as in "I fancy that bloke!"

Mate (noun): A pal, a chum, a bosom bud. All Saints is a group of musical mates.

Row (verb): To fight, squabble, feud. "Me and Nat row all the time, sometimes over the smallest things," says Nic. "It can be nuclear war."

Some Saints Suggestions

When the girls begin their trek across the States, they should sample key hot spots currently spinning their CD:

Trees in Dallas is located in the ultra-hip Deep Ellum section of downtown Big D. Teens (you gotta be at least seventeen to get in) come here to hear the loud, louder, and loudest local bands. They're the first to spin the hot new CD du jour—so ya know All Saints was on their playlist.

The Church in Cleveland. The name alone should send a signal to the Saints that this is a club they'd love. Don't let the mile-long line outside scare you off: The fresh remixes are divine, and worth the wait. You have to be at least eighteen, with an ID, to party here.

Stuck in the States?

Even if you ain't a Saint, you can head to their U.S. haunts:

Bowery Bar in NYC. The East Village's ultrahip hangout boasts great eats. One of the first stops when the band visited the city.

Melrose Ave. in LA for funky fashions.

The Cameron Public House in downtown Toronto (Hey, Canada may not be in the States, but it is Nic and Nat's homebase) frequently plays "I Know Where It's At" and has reported several Saints sightings. It's a down-and-dirty R&B/alternative club where local kids congregate. You've got to be nineteen or older to get in most days, but anyone can go to feast on their scrumptious Sunday brunch.

Chapter 3
The British Invasion

*N*ow that you know the Saints' score, it may be time to give props to those who came before. If it weren't for these Brits leading the way, All Saints might never have been as big as they are today. Brush up on your Brit rock history, so when Shaz, Mel, Nic, and Nat arrive in the States, you can impress 'em with your knowledge of their native land's music makers!

The Beatles

The Fab Four were the brainchild of John Lennon, a rebellious Liverpool teen with a passion for rock 'n' roll. He and his high school pal Paul McCartney were just messing around with some guitars and decided they'd form a band called The Quarrymen (Paul asked his bud George Harrison to jam with them). After a name change to The Silver Beatles (they later shortened it) and several rounds of musical chairs with band members (Stu and Pete are out; Ringo's in), the band's sound began to spread. Unlike the doo-wop warbling of most '50s bands, the Beatles were brasher, bolder, and more innovative—like nothing teens had ever heard before. A local record store manager, Brian Epstein, caught their act and asked to manage them. He later helped them find their first label, Parlophone, and they signed up with producer George Martin. In 1963, "Please Please Me" topped the British charts and the Liverpudlian lads appeared on *The Ed Sullivan Show*. World-wide Beatlemania had begun! From screaming fans for *Sgt. Pepper* to *A Hard Day's Night* (the granddaddy of music videos!) on the big screen, the group was one of the major influences on music this century and credited with beginning what became known as The British Invasion.

Way-cool Web Sites on the Beatles

http://www.mplcommunications.com/
Paul's official page

http://www.earthcorp.com/beatlezone

http://www.thecore.com/~mike/faq.htm

http://www.pathfinder.com/Life/beatles/beatles.html

http://www.hollywoodandvine.com/Anthology/

http://imusic.com/showcase/rock/beatles.html

http://www.geocities.com/SunsetStrip/Palms/5005/

The Animals

This band roared onto the music scene in the '60s with an R&B sound that they perfected in their native Newcastle. Alan Price, John Steel, Eric Burdon, Bryan "Chas" Chandler, and Hilton Valentine recorded hit

after hit ("Baby Let Me Take You Home,"
"House of the Rising Sun," "I'm Crying,"
"Don't Let Me Be Misunderstood," and "We've
Gotta Get Out of This Place"), clawing their
way to the top of the pop charts. Despite
their success, the band's relationship was
frequently on the rocks. Sadly, their 1966 hit
"Don't Bring Me Down" marked the end of
the original Animals. They reunited in 1976 for
an album called *Before We Were So Rudely
Interrupted* (way-apropos title, no?), which
picked up right where they had left off a
decade before. In 1983, they banded together
once again to record *Ark*, and a world tour
followed. But the end of the year and the
hectic tour schedule, it was clear that this
harmony wasn't for keeps: the quintet said
their final farewells to fans and to more than
twenty years of turning out tunes.

Way-cool Web Sites for Animals Info

http://imusic.com/cgi-bin/bbs/bbs.cgi?x=
animals
http://www2.netcom.com/~bassboy/
The official American homepage

The Rolling Stones

Okay—maybe modesty wasn't their finest quality. But when the Rolling Stones dubbed themselves "The World's Greatest Rock 'n' Roll Band" in the 1960s, they weren't too far from the truth. Mick Jagger met Keith Richards as kids at Dartford Maypole County Primary School—and even back then they had a plan to revolutionize rock. Unlike the Merseybeat of the Beatles, the Stones sound was grittier. Macho Mick liked to strut around the stage in skintight pants, while Keith and Brian Jones wrote wailing guitar harmonies. Bill Wyman and Charlie Watts completed the team as the band perfected its "walk on the wild side" attitude. Early in 1964, their cover of Buddy Holly's "Not Fade Away," shot to the number-three spot. They followed it with a string of hits, including "Time Is On My Side " and "(I Can't Get No) Satisfaction." Troubled times followed with several members of the band getting busted for drug use and their albums slipping out of critics' and fans' favor. But in 1980 they came back with a vengeance, releasing the sizzling single "Start Me Up." Their *Tattoo You* album spent nine weeks at number one. The Stones rolled into the '90s with *Voodoo Lounge*, *Rock & Roll Circus*, and last year's *Bridges to Babylon* albums, and today continue to blow away standing-room-only crowds.

Way-cool Web Sites for the Stones

http://www.the-rolling-stones.com

The official site

http://www.stonesworld.com

Another claiming to be official

http://www.stonesbazaar.com

Mega merchandise

The Who

Pete Townshend and John Entwistle met while attending high school in the Shepherd's Bush area of London. As teens, they played in a Dixieland band together, John on trumpet and Pete picking a banjo. But they were rock at heart. The band they formed shaped the mod movement of the mid-'60s, with a sound that was both explosive and chaotic. Pete and John, along with Keith Moon and Roger Daltrey, created teenage anthems for an era, including "The Kids Are Alright" and "My Generation." While most bands stuck to what would sell, The Who recorded ambitious rock operas such as *Tommy* and *Quadrophenia*. They disbanded in the early '80s, but reunited several times in the late '80s and '90s to tour the States.

Way-cool Web Sites for the Who

> http://www.yo.rim.or.jp/~f-toru/index.html
> http://imusic.com/showcase/rock/who.html
> http://www.eden.com/~thewho/
> http://members.aol.com/WhoLive/

index.html Complete concert guide

British Invasion Pop Quiz

1. What is Ringo Starr's real name?

(a) Richard Starkey

(b) Richard Ringo

(c) Richard Starr

(d) Ricky Ring

2. What was the last song The Beatles recorded?

    (a) "Let It Be"

    (b) "Yesterday"

    (c) "I Wanna Hold Your Hand"

    (d) "I Me Mine"

3. What guitar god played on George's "While My Guitar Gently Weeps?"

    (a) Eddie Van Halen

    (b) Eric Clapton

    (c) Richie Sambora

    (d) Stu Sutcliffe

4. What was the original title for "Yesterday"?

    (a) "Scrambled Eggs"

    (b) "Tomorrow"

    (c) "I'm Not Half the Man I Used to Be"

    (d) "Rock Me Amadeus"

5. What keyboardist joined the Animals after they reunited?

    (a) Billy Joel

    (b) Zoot Money

    (c) Elton John

    (d) Barry Manilow

6. What school did Mick Jagger once attend?

    (a) The London School of Economics

    (b) Horace Mann

    (c) Liverpool Academy of Music

    (d) Oxford University

7. The Rolling Stones got their name from:

    (a) Rolling Stone Street in London

    (b) the back of a cereal box

    (c) the name of a British sitcom

    (d) a Muddy Waters song

8. What Who album became a Broadway musical?

    (a) *Tommy*

    (b) *Who's Next*

    (c) *Oklahoma!*

    (d) *Quadrophenia*

9. What did Pete Townshend study while the band struggled to get a break?

    (a) veterinary medicine

    (b) journalism

    (c) art

    (d) basket weaving

10. What was The Who's first top ten hit in America?

    (a) "I Can See for Miles and Miles"

    (b) "Pinball Wizard"

    (c) "I Can't Explain"

    (d) "Anyway, Anyhow, Anywhere"

ANSWERS: 1. a; 2. d; 3. b; 4. a; 5. b; 6. a; 7. d; 8. a; 9. c; 10. a.

Chapter 4

The Babes in the Band/The Wild One, Nicole

*N*ic at night is a sight to behold: the beautiful blonde loves to dance and party till the sun comes up.

It's perfectly understandable when you consider the 24-year-old's childhood: Nic was a total nerd. "A major dweeb," she laughs. "With greasy hair and rat tails. All of my clothes were hand-me-downs from Nat. I was never chased by boys."

Things have certainly changed. According to the Saints, Nic's now the one who gets all the attention. Why then has it been two years since she's had a boyfriend? The British tabs tell her tale: a two-year engagement ended painfully, and now her ex is revealing every detail of their romance to the papers.

What's a girl to do? Get over it! Nic's not one to dwell on the past, but you can bet she won't make the same mistake twice. "Boys are drawn to her like bees to honey," says Mel. "She's the best of us at getting guys. She knows how to work it."

Working a job, however, is not her specialty. "I've been sacked from every employment I've ever had. I was an ice cream vendor in New York once and the umbrella on the cart came crashing down on my head. Over $90 in ice cream was stolen while I was out cold on the sidewalk. The only thing I've ever been a success at is All Saints." Lucky for us.

Name: *Nicole Marie Appleton*

A.k.a.: *Nic, Tequila Queen, The Fonz or Fonzie*

DOB: *December 7, 1974*

Height: *5'6"*

Weight: *113 lbs.*

Eyes: *Brown*

Hair: *Blond*

Original addresses: *Canada and Camden, London, where she lived with her dad*

Her heritage: *Canadian and English*

Her hood today: *Belsize Park, London*

Junk food junkie: *Nic can't say no to a snack attack at Micky D's. Her faves are the fries ("greasy and great!").*

Feline fan: *Nic has two cats, Nathan and Nathana, who live in her studio flat. "They're more dependable than any man."*

Forget the fibs: *Nic says she'll despise anyone who tells lies.*

Catwoman: *Nic has a tattoo—the symbol for the Year of the Tiger—just below the belt.*

Life of the party: *"I'm the soul of the group. Even when they're in a bad mood, I know how to liven them up."*

Material girl: *Nic does a mean Madonna impression and once passed* *herself off as the pop star.*

Recent Romeo: *Robbie Williams of Take That. Nic met him on her birthday. "I can't bear to be away from him."*

Camera shy: *"It hurts me that my private life has been made so public."*

Saintly? *"Depends on the day."*

Chapter 5
The Babes in the Band/The Homegirl, Melanie

*T*hink spending an evening at home with the folks is a downer? Well, don't tell that to Mel. Despite the Saints' success, the 23-year-old loves living at home with her mum and pop in London. "I'm totally dependent on them again," she admits. "I think I might be living my life backwards—by this time next year I'll be an embryo."

Mel and her folks are pretty tight, maybe because they helped see her through some tough times in her life. "I had scoliosis growing up," she admits. "I went through some painful surgery to correct it. But I think dealing with it made me a stronger person."

Her family is also the reason she discovered music. Her French mom and English dad were hippies who took Mel to the Glastonbury Festival—England's answer to Woodstock—when she was just nine months old. "I had a pretty unconventional upbringing," she says. Her family had their own business and moved around quite a bit, living at different times in France and even living in a T-shirt factory in London ("we had nowhere else to live"). She grew up listening to their favorite groups: "Lots of Led Zeppelin and R&B."

Her parents pushed her into the spotlight when she was just six years old. "They made me stand on the hood of the car and play the viola," Mel recalls. "I guess you could say musical performance is in my blood."

Name: *Melanie Blatt*

A.k.a.: *Mel-odie, Blatt Fink. "Shaznay calls me Smell. Nic and Nat call me Bucket."*

DOB: *March 25, 1975*

Height: *5'3"*

Weight: *108 lbs.*

Eyes: *Hazel*

Hair: *Brown*

Original addresses: *England and France*

Her hood today: *She lives with her family in Ladbrook Grove, London.*

Her heritage: *French and English*

Julia Child wannabe: *"I'm into cooking and watching cookery programs on the telly."*

Dance fever: *Mel originally wanted to be a ballet dancer, but her back problems derailed that dream.*

Tattoo times two: *She has a blue dragon that curls around her ribcage and a musical score on her shoulder (how apropos!). "I was a bit pissed off about that one," she admits. "There are five musical staves in a score and the guy put in six."*

The hills are alive: *"Watching Julie Andrews in The Sound of Music made me want to sing."*

Fave holiday: *A recent trip to the Big*

Apple. "We ordered in pizza at the hotel and watched *Scream* on a huge-screen TV. Then we went to the Backstreet Boys party in Rockefeller Center, met Aaliyah, and had loads of fun."

Mel's man: *A beau ("no comment!") with whom she spent Christmas. Her only hint:* "He's also used to traveling with a tour manager." *Hmmmm . . . a fellow musician?*

A regular Girl Scout: "I am always prepared. I'm the organizer of the group. I've always got what people need in my bag."

Too close for comfort? *Fans often send mail to Mel's home address.* "How do they get this info anyway? It's freaky!"

Saintly? "I'm a good girl. I'm not very good at flirting—I need to take lessons from Nicky."

Chapter 6
The Babes in the Band/The Word Woman, Shaz

*N*othing like a rocky relationship to set you on the road to stardom: Shaz was in the midst of a breakup with a bloke when she decided to put her feelings down on paper. "Never ever" had she felt so low—sound familiar? "Well," laughs the 23-year-old, "at least something good came of that split."

The Saints are the first to tell you that Shaz is the brains behind the band. She spent years laying background vocals in exchange for studio time, all the while picking up the info and technique she needed to write and record.

"People say I'm smart," she admits, "but I don't know about that. Sometimes I can be terribly absentminded. I once left a holdall full of my underwear in a taxi. Can you imagine losing your knickers in a cab?"

One of her first jobs was working in a men's clothing store. "I did it for three weeks as a favor to a friend," she says. "I was in the shoe department and I spent the whole day giving out refunds because the shoes always fell apart."

Although she is terribly proud of Shaznay, there are times when her mom would have preferred for Shaz to stay in a more traditional job. Sometimes when she sees her daughter dancing in an All Saints video, she'll raise her eyebrows and say, "Oooooh, Shaznay!" Shaznay's good-natured response: Better get used to it, Mum!

Name: *Shaznay Tricia Lewis*

A.k.a.: *Bart ("because people say I sound like Bart Simpson when I rap").*

DOB: *October 14, 1975*

Her original address: *England*

Her hood today: *Islington, London, with her mum and little sis. Her best friend still lives next door.*

Her heritage: *Half Jamaican, half Barbadian*

Height: *5'7"*

Weight: *120 lbs.*

Eyes: *Dark brown*

Hair: *Brown*

Her ideal gal pal: *Pollyanna or Aretha Franklin. "I only like upbeat, positive people. I'm also big on R-E-S-P-E-C-T."*

Nix being nasty: *"I can't stand when people are rude or cop an attitude."*

Music's a must: *"I always sang at school, wrote little poems, rapped for my friends. Even if I ended up working in a shop, I would have been singing on the side."*

Tin grin: *Shaz just had braces removed!*

Kid crush: *"I was a huge New Kids on the Block fan. I was so excited to visit*

Boston, their home, when we came to the U.S."

Couch potato: *Her favorite thing to do on a day off? "Kick up my feet on the sofa."*

Tough customer: *"I can handle myself, you know, so watch out."*

Wrong words: *"My mum's favorite song on our album is 'Under the Bridge.' It was tough telling her I didn't write it!"*

Betcha didn't know: *Shaz is shy. "I'm the quiet one of the group. I can be a bit mad like the others sometimes, but usually I'm the most serious."*

Saintly? *"I'm quite religious, but I do some little things I know are bad!"*

Chapter 7
The Babes in the Band/The Big Sis, Natalie

"*There* she goes, Mother Hen!" jokes Nic about her All Saints sister. Nat never minds the needling. She's proud of her maternal instincts and the fact that she's a single mum to a 5-year-old daughter, Rachael—as well as to all the girls in the band. She's the one they turn to for advice. "They're lucky—I almost didn't join up," the 25-year-old admits. She feared becoming a Saint would keep her away from her little girl. Fortunately, her folks stepped in to look after her. For the Appleton sibs, it turned out to be a double blessing: their parents, who had been divorced, got back together after a fifteen-year split. "It's a decision I'm glad I made," Nat says. "Sometimes you gotta just trust your instincts."

Nat can tell you firsthand that seeing isn't always believing. When tabloids ran wild stories about her she was hurt, but managed to hang in there. Her ex-husband told the papers that Nat had had a nose job, among other things, and that she was still married to him.

"It didn't surprise me that the stories came out," she asserts. "The truth is we flew to the States together and he couldn't get a job because he was English. We had a daughter, so I was determined to make it work for her sake. . . . He ran away and I came back to the U.K. and had the marriage annulled. End of story."

Anything else? "Oh yeah—I broke my nose when I was thirteen and had to have it operated on." Next time you want the reason and rhyme, go straight to the source!

Name: *Natalie Jane Appleton*

A.k.a.: *Nat, Naaatalie*

DOB: *May 14, 1973*

Original addresses: *Mississagua, Canada, and upstate New York*

Her hood today: *Camden, London, where she lives with her mum*

Her heritage: *Canadian and English*

Height: *5'5"*

Weight: *112 lbs.*

Eyes: *Green*

Hair: *Blond*

Scream queen: *"I like reading scary, sick stories. Stephen King is my hero."*

School ties: *Mel knew Nat from class and asked her to be in the band.*

Boss lady: *"I push everyone around and tell them what to do. It's that big sister thing."*

Glamor girl: *When Nat was fifteen, her mum used to make her up to look a little older so that she could sing in hotels. "I'd* sing anything—'Tie a Yellow Ribbon Round the Old Oak Tree' was always a popular request."

Snow business: *When her parents divorced, Nat was separated from her sis, Nic. She was just seven when she left Canada and remembers nothing about it, except for all the snow.*

Sorry, sis: *"I once cut off all of Nic's hair with big garden scissors 'cause I wanted a brother."*

Worrywart: *"I'm the kind of person who worries about anything—whether I'm singing for one person or thousands."*

Childhood chum: *Nat and Mel went to the Sylvia Young Theater School in London with Emma "Baby Spice" Bunton. "She's a couple of years younger than me. When you're in school, you don't hang out with the young kids. She was such a cute little kid that I would say hello to her now and then."*

"Don't call us, we'll call you": *Before joining the band Nic and Nat came to the*

U.S. trying to break into the biz. "We got doors slammed in our faces and all that fun stuff."

Saintly? "Sinner, definitely. I'm a heartbreaker. If I get bored with a boy I dump him. I once went out with this guy in high school for just one day. He was so cut up, he didn't go out with anyone for a year after that."

Chapter 8
All Saints Sez...

*A*s brilliant as this band is at writing lyrics, you know they'd come up with the coolest of quotables!

Flirting 101: *"My technique is to slant my mouth, squint my eyes and smile. Never fails!"*—Nic

Spice speak: *"We're not fighting with the Spice Girls like the British tabloids have reported. I guess it's just that the papers want to build the hype. Look, they [the Spice Girls] know what the press is about. They've been there and seen it. They know it's all a bunch of bull."*—Nat

Kiss and tell: *"We blab to each other the day after a date. All the dirty, delicious details."*—Shaz

Mother knows best: *"It's hard when you're home for a day and your mum tells you to do the washing up."*—Shaz

Mother knows best, part II: *"Our mothers are the greatest women alive. They're the generation who fought for us."*—Mel told *Spin*

Taking it in stride: *"I really didn't expect any of this. It's amazing to think there are so many people out there who like what we're doing. I suppose I should be reveling in it, but I just can't."*—Shaz

Their dream date: *"Jerry Springer. He's our hero."*—Nat told *EW*

The Big Time: *"We had no money, and we didn't have jobs, because we wanted to focus on our music. We were at the point where we had to make it, or else."*—Shaz told *Jump*

"We used to watch Wham! on Top of the Pops and dream of being in the audience. Now we're on the show and the audience is

The four heavenly honeys take five. (©1998, Jill Douglas Redferns/Retna)

All Saints . . . the miracle act.
(©1997, John Marshall /Redferns/Retna)

"Never ever" leave without a smile.
(©1997, Terry Williams/London Features)

The ever-huggable Shaz and Mel.
(©1998, Colin Bell/Retna)

Cuddling for the camera.
(©1997, Ilpo Musto/London Features)

**The girls send a message
out to fans over the airwaves.**
(©1998, Justin Thomas/All Action/Retna)

All Saints devotees flock to see the divine divas. (©1998, Sheena Haywood All Action/Retna)

All Saints, all girls, all power.
(©1997, David Fisher/London Features)

Behind the scenes with the beauty queens.
(©1997, Sean Smith/Retna)

Nicole is as happy signing autographs as she is signing record deals.
(©1998, Sheena Haywood/All Action/Retna)

After taking home the gold at the 1998 Brit Awards, the quadruple platinum Saints are united to take on the world. (©1998, David Fisher/London Features)

"Yeah, bay-bee!" All Saints bond with the International Man of Mystery, Mike Meyers. (©1998, Kevin Mazur/London Features)

Four-part harmony never sounded
better than with . . .

Nicole

Melanie

Shaznay

Natalie

(©1997, James McCauley/Retna)

(©1997, James McCauley/Retna)

(©1997, James McCauley/Retna)

(©1998, Sheena Haywood/All Action/Retna)

Name: Melanie R. Blatt
Aka: Mel-odie, Blatt Fink.
"Shaznay calls me Smell. Nic
and Nat call me Bucket."
DOB: March 25, 1975
Height: 5' 3"
Eyes: hazel
Hair: brown
Original addresses: England
and France
Tattoo times two: She has a
blue dragon that curls around
her ribcage and a musical
score on her shoulder (how
apropos!).
A regular Girl Scout: "I am
always prepared. I'm the organizer of the group. I've always
got what people need in my
bag."
Saint or sinner? "I'm a good
girl. I'm not very good at flirting—I need to take lessons
from Nicky."

Name: Nicole Marie Appleton
Aka: Nic, The Fonz or Fonzie
DOB: December 7, 1974
Height: 5' 6"
Eyes: brown
Hair: blond
Her hood today: Belsize Park,
London
Catwoman: Nic has a tattoo—the
symbol for the Year of the
Tiger—plunging below the belt.
Life of the party: "I'm the soul of
the group. Even when they're in
a bad mood, I know how to liven
them up."
Saint or sinner? "Depends on
the day."

Name: Natalie Jane Appleton
Aka: Nat, Naaatalie
DOB: May 14, 1975
Her hood today: Camden,
London, where she lives with her
mum
Height: 5' 5"
Eyes: green
Hair: blond
Scream queen: "I like reading
scary, sick stories. Stephen King
is my hero."
Boss lady: "I push everyone
around and tell them what to do.
It's that big sister thing."
Sorry, Sis: "I once cut off all of
Nic's hair with big garden scis-
sors 'cause I wanted a brother."
Saint or sinner? "Sinner,
definitely. I'm a heartbreaker."

Name: Shaznay Tricia Lewis
Aka: Bart, "because people say I
sound like Bart Simpson when I
rap."
DOB: October 14, 1975
Original address: England
Height: 5' 7"
Eyes: dark brown
Hair: brown
Tin grin: Shaz just had braces
removed!
Betcha didn't know: Shaz is shy.
"I'm the quiet one of the group. I
can be a bit mad like the others
sometimes, but usually I'm the
most serious."
Saint or sinner? "I'm quite reli-
gious, but I do some little things
I know are bad!"

watching us!"—Nat

Mind games: *"You have to think for yourself."*—Mel

"I think for Mel all the time."—Nic

Hip chick: *"I like to wear bright-colored tops to draw the eye away from my hips and lower half."*—Shaz

Keepin' it real: *"Our first video is an in-your-face intro to who we are. No flying penguins or anything fancy."*—Nat told *Seventeen*

And What the Critics Say About All Saints

"Now that the Spice Girls are looking bland, and most American groups are Go-Go-gone, who's left to fill the hearts, ears, and Web pages? All Saints are here to get a rise out of you. A fine debut . . ."—*Maxim*

"The cookie toughs . . . deliver flowing harmonies heavily steeped in American beats. The album is full of fun. . . ."—*Vibe*

"All Saints are so smooth, they sound like the handiwork of a savvy music marketer—

which, surprisingly, they are not. By the time their album hits stores, rest assured, radio and MTV will have beaten their singles to death. . . ."—*The New York Post*

"There are certain things in life you can be sure of, that it will rain on bank holidays and that All Saints are going to be massive. . . ." —*Melody Maker*

"From the UK, comes four, funky females, who are bringing a smart, soulful spirit straight to the top of the pop charts worldwide. It's All Saints' Day, and that's all right by us!"—*The Face*

Chapter 9
The Playlist

"*A*ll Saints have the ability for turning out melodic, meaningful songs that cling to your senses for dear life. To merely describe them as 'catchy' would be like calling St. Paul's Cathedral a nice little church. All Saints don't have to try too hard to impress—the songs do the job for them."—London Records

Their music is hard to put your finger on: part hip-hop, part soul, part street beat, part get-on-your-feet. It's house. It's happening. It's hot.

"We have so many different influences, that it took us a long time to work on our material," says Shaz. "There weren't that many British female bands out, and the ones that were out, we didn't want to be like them."

So they put their heads—and their musical tastes—together, creating something all their own. "We range from R&B and soul to swing and pop," adds Mel. "You can hear all those colors in what we do."

Shaz's sure bets: Rap, Aretha, Bob Marley, Tina Turner, Busta Rhymes, and UB40. "I like up-tempo tracks with big beats," she says. And she writes most of the lyrics herself. "I like to be honest about what I write."

Nat's musical notes: Rock and funk— hence her suggestion of covering Red Hot Chili Peppers' "Under the Bridge." Her other faves? Alternative bands such as Prodigy and The Verve.

Mel's muses: Stevie Wonder and Prince.

Nic's picks: Any CDs from Robbie Williams, Oasis or Blur, Janet Jackson, Beck, L.L. Cool J., and another cool J—Judy Garland! "I loved Whitney Houston growing up," she told *Rolling Stone Online*. "My first album that I ever bought was Madonna's *True Blue*. My first single was 'Let's Get Physical' from Olivia Newton-John. Then I moved to the States and I got into hip-hop and rap . . . like 2 Live Crew."

Tracks Facts

MCA has a three-album publishing deal with the group (which means we've got two more to be psyched for!).

1. **Never Ever** (R. Jazzayeri/S. Mather/
   S. Lewis)
   Produced by Cameron McVey and Magnus Fiennes
   Mix Engineered by Niven Garland
   Additional production by Rickidy Raw and Mystro

"I wrote it when I was rock bottom," says Shaz. "There was a lot of hurt, and it all came crashing down for me at the same time Mel was feeling the same way, so she could relate to it. We were so depressed when I wrote it that we couldn't listen to it for months." Their label calls it a "gospel-tinged heartbreaker" in the tradition of the Shangri-Las' "Past, Present and Future."

2. **Bootie Call** (S. Lewis/K. Gordon)
   Produced by Karl Gordon
   Engineered by Marcellus Fernandes
   Additional keyboard programming by
   Sean Cox
   Drum programming and instruments by
   Karl Gordon

This is Shaznay having some fun with us. "It's just me and my perverted mind," Shaz says of this sassy song. "Nah, not really! . . . I wanted to give [men] some of their own medicine."

3. **I Know Where It's At** (K. Gordon/
   S. Lewis/P. Griffen/W. Becker/D. Fagen)
   Produced by Cameron McVey, Magnus
   Fiennes, and Karl Gordon
   Contains elements of "The Fez"
   performed by Steely Dan
   Drum loop produced by Karl Gordon

The group's mantra—and debut dance track. Locked in the studio, the girls decided to create their own party. "The song is about having fun," says Mel.

4. **Under the Bridge** (Flea/A. Kiedis/
   C. Smith/J. Frusciante)

Produced by Nellee Hooper and Karl
Gordon
Mixed by Nellee Hooper
Mix engineered by Jim Abbisi

Includes samples from the original Red
Hot Chili Peppers' recording and the Rampage
recording "Wild for Da Night."

Why choose a song by an LA rock band?
"'Cause that's the last thing people would
expect us to do," says Shaz.

5. **Heaven** (N. Appleton/N. Appleton/
   S. Lewis/M. Blatt/C. McVey/M. Fiennes)
   Produced by Cameron McVey and
   Magnus Fiennes
   Mixed by John Benson
   Engineered by Ruadhri Cushnan

The producers pitch this one as "a low-
slung piece of sultry funk." Each of the band's
four members added an impromptu verse
about standing at the gates of heaven.

6. **Alone** (K. Gordon/S. Lewis)
   Produced by Karl Gordon
   Drum programming and keyboards by
   Karl Gordon

Additional keyboards by John Benson

If something's wrong, say the Saints in this tune, better make your feelings known. . . .

7. **If You Want to Party (I Found Lovin')**
   (J. Flippin/M. Walker)
   Produced by Johnny Douglas

"The Best Party Track in Town" and a funkadelic dance fest!

8. **Trapped** (N. Henry/K. Gibbs/M. Blatt)
   Produced by Neville Henry, Karen Gibbs, and John Benson
   Mixed by John Benson
   Engineered by Ruadhri Cushnan

About a lady who's lost her way. The Saints' message? Get off your butt or regret the day.

9. **Beg** (J. Douglas/S. Lewis/J. Benson)
   Produced by Johnny Douglas and John Benson
   Mixed by John Benson
   Engineered by Ruadhri Cushnan

Hell hath no fury like a Saint who's been scorned! But Shaz insists this isn't her attempt to get even with an ex. "It's just a message to people in the industry who didn't want to know us when we were struggling and then wanted to be best mates with us when we got our deal. They know who they are."

10. **Lady Marmalade** (B. Crewe/K. Nolan)
Produced by Johnny Douglas, Neville Henry, Karen Gibbs, and John Benson
Mixed by John Benson and Ruadhri Cushnan

This little ditty was a chart-topper in 1975. The girls give it a '90s groove.

11. **Take the Key** (S. Lewis/K. Gordon/ K. Robinson/N. Robinson)
Produced by Karl Gordon
Additional keyboards by Cyril McNammon
Featuring a sample from the Audio Two recording "Top Billin"

Shaz sez this is her fave song on the album. "It's very happy," she told *Jump*. "It's about falling in love."

12. **War of Nerves** (C. McVey/M. Fiennes/ S. Lewis/N. Appleton/N. Appleton)
Produced by Cameron McVey and Magnus Fiennes

Mixed by Niven Garland

Shaz wrote this lyric the weekend Princess Di was killed. "Everyone suddenly got scared because it was a shock. It brought the subject of death closer to a lot of people who hadn't experienced it."

Instant Replay

Sure, you spin their CD night and day. But how much do you know about it?

1. What two Saints thank their fans in the CD's booklet?

   (a) Mel and Shaz

   (b) Nic and Nat

   (c) Nic and Shaz

   (d) Nat and Mel

2. What song is a cover of a Patti LaBelle classic?

   (a) "Trapped"

   (b) "Under the Bridge"

   (c) "Lady Marmalade"

   (d) "If You Want to Party"

3. What song did *all* the girls write?

    (a) "I Know Where It's At"

    (b) "War of Nerves"

    (c) "Heaven"

    (d) "Beg"

4. In "Lady Marmalade," what does *"Voulez-vous couchez avec moi"* mean?

    (a) "Please pass the Grey Poupon."

    (b) "Do you have a light, mister?"

    (c) "Do you want to sleep with me?"

    (d) "Could you move over and stop hogging the couch?"

5. In "Never Ever," which way do the Saints *not* recommend Romeo reply?

    (a) over the Internet

    (b) in a letter

    (c) on the phone

    (d) in person

6. What city does "Under the Bridge" take place in?

    (a) London

(b) Los Angeles

(c) New York

(d) Chicago

7. What song insists "Don't deny, don't be shy, just come around?"

   (a) "Alone"

   (b) "Take the Key"

   (c) "Trapped"

   (d) "I Know Where It's At"

8. Who designed the look of the album?

   (a) All Saints

   (b) Donna Karan

   (c) Stuart Spalding and Lee Swillingham

   (d) John Benson and Johnny Douglas

9. Who took the photo of the Saints on their album cover?

   (a) Sean Ellis

   (b) John Benson

   (c) Herb Ritts

   (d) Stacy Polsky

10. What song, does Shaz say, makes her

mom blush every time she sings it?

    (a) "Beg"

    (b) "Bootie Call"

    (c) "Under the Bridge"

    (d) "Heaven"

ANSWERS: 1. a; 2. c; 3. c; 4. c; 5. a; 6. b; 7. d; 8. c; 9. a; 10. b.

Change of Tune

"We were going to call ourselves Shifty," Nic reveals. Another try—All Saints 1.9.7.5. (when just a duo, Mel and Shaz wanted to add the year they were born). Most musical groups have second thoughts. Can you match these bands to their new and improved *noms*?

1. The Bangles	(a) Johnny and the Moondogs
2. The Cure	(b) Composition of Sound
3. Salt-n-Pepa	(c) The Warlocks
4. U2	(d) The Primettes
5. The Grateful Dead	(e) Carl and the Passions

6. The Beatles   (f) Goat Band

7. The Bee Gees   (g) The Rattlesnakes

8. The Supremes   (h) Supernature

9. Depeche Mode   (i) Feedback

10. The Beach Boys   (j) Supersonic Bangs

ANSWERS: 1. j; 2. f; 3. h; 4. i; 5. c; 6. a; 7. g; 8. d; 9. b; 10. e.

What's in a Name?

So the Saints snagged their name from a street sign in London. Ever wonder where these groups got their ID's?

ABBA: An acronym made up of the first letters of each band member's name (Agnetha, Benny, Bjorn, and Anni-Frid).

Duran Duran: Nabbed from the name of the villain in the '60s sci-fi flick *Barbarella*, starring Jane Fonda.

Hole: Courtney Love liked a line in the Greek tragedy *Medea*: "There's a hole burning deep inside of me."

Pearl Jam: Named for Eddie Vedder's gram, Pearl.

UB40: The name of the Brit unemployment benefit card.

Soundgarden: A beach sculpture in Seattle that whistles in the wind.

The Chick Clique

The Saints are far from the first girl group to hit it big. Just a few to give a listen to:

Bananarama: An '80s British import consisting of Sara Dallin, Keren Woodward, and Siobhan Fahey. They had 29 hit singles, including "Cruel Summer" and "Venus."

En Vogue: "Funky Divas" Dawn Robinson, Cindy Herron, Maxine Jones, and Terry Ellis teamed in 1990. Their biggest hits were the pulsating tracks "Free Your Mind" and "Whatta Man."

The Go-Gos: In the late '70s and early '80s, singer Belinda Carlisle and bandmates Jane Wiedlin, Margot Olaverra, Gina Shock, and Charlotte Caffey churned out chirpy hits including "We Got the Beat" and "Our Lips Are Sealed" before calling it quits. Belinda went solo.

The Shangri-Las: All Saints are often compared to this 1960s band. "I've never even heard them," Shaz admits. Another sister act—Mary and Betty Weiss hooked up with twins Marge and Mary Ann Ganser. Their big hit (they added motorcycle sound effects) was "Leader of the Pack."

Spice Girls: Wonder what all the buzz is about? Check out Melanie Brown, Melanie Chisholm, Victoria Adams, Emma Bunton, and Geri Halliwell's (before her split from the band) boogie-based sound. "Wannabe," their first single, is a winner.

TLC: In 1992, Tionne "T-Boz" Watkins, Lisa "Left-Eye" Lopes, and Rozanda "Chilli" Thomas made their debut in the urban arena. The homegirls' hits included "Ain't Too Proud to Beg," "Baby Baby Baby," and "What About Your Friends."

And this list just scratches the surface of successful all-female groups. For further 411, some sites to scout:

Bananarama:

http://www.curb.com/Artists/br.html

http://itre.ncsu.edu/jay/brama/

http://www.missioncontrol.co.uk/banbiog.htm

http://www.geocities.com/CollegePark/Union/6146/bananarama.html

http://www.bananaramaweb.com/

En Vogue:

http://www.elektra.com/randb_club/en_vogue/en_vogue_press.html

http://www.geocities.com/SunsetStrip/Lounge/6495/

Go-Gos:

http://www.yahoo.com/Entertainment/Music/Artists/By_Genre/Rock_and_Pop/Go_Gos/

http://www.ee.surrey.ac.uk/contrib/music/go-gos/go-gos.html

Shangri-Las:

http://www.crl.com/~tsimon/shangri.htm

http://www.in-your-ear.com/listings/ear/a7a2_132.htm

http://home.ica.net/~phil/thegirls/shangri.htm

Spice Girls:

http://fej.simplenet.com/spice/spice.html Desktop theme page

http://www.geocities.com/SunsetStrip/Stage/6101

http://www.geocities.com/SunsetStrip/Arena/9424/index.htm

http://www.wallofsound.com/artists/spicegirls/index.html

http://www.virginrecords.com/spice_girls/spice.html The Official site

http://www.globalmedia.co.uk/spice/

http://www.unfurled.com/ultimate_artists/spice_girls/index.html

TLC:

http://www.yahoo.com/Entertainment/Music/Artists/By_Genre/Rap_and_Hip_Hop/TLC/

http://www.mbnet.mb.ca/~alouie/tlc.htm

http://www.Geocities.com/Hollywood/2320/

Chapter 10
The Long and Winding Road

*G*lobetrotting has its good points and bad. Just ask All Saints:

Nat: "I discovered in Germany that I hate their breakfasts," she told *Rolling Stone Online*. "It's 6 A.M., and they serve you brie and salami and black pumpernickel bread."

Nicky: "It's horrible! Hello! What happened to sausage sandwiches and cereal?"

Mel: "These Polish fans knew everything about me. Like the color of my underwear that day."

Shaz: "It's surreal, you know? They were

hanging out front of our hotel with cameras."

The crowd-friendly band seems to take all the fuss in stride, turning things around by asking their fans a question or two in reply.

Bizarre breakfasts and autograph hounds aside, is being on a promo and concert tour as totally cool as it sounds? Come along for the ride and see for yourself. . . .

Here, There, and Everywhere

Okay, you've recorded the hottest album on the planet. But it's gonna bomb unless you get people to buy it. How do you do that? You get in their face and erase all the competition! It's hard to resist giving a new band's beat a try when every radio, TV station, newspaper, and magazine is calling them the biggest thing since sliced bread. The All Saints—savvy sistas that they are—immediately took their act on the road. Along with Robbie Williams and Dublin's own Boyzone and OTT boy bands, All Saints topped the bill at a concert in the Point Theatre beside the River Liffey in Dublin. The show, called A Pop Extravaganza, also had some help from the Spice Girls: they loaned their public address system and lighting equipment to the organizers. They've also hit Japan, Australia, Poland, Germany, and of course, the U.S. of A. with their funky live show. They posed for teen magazines. They chatted online. They appeared on *Saturday Night Live* and *Regis & Kathie Lee*.

The upside: You get to see new cities and sights and meet new people. Rack up those frequent flyer miles! Reservations in the hottest clubs, hotels, and restaurants at the snap of your fingers. Your name in all the local headlines and people recognizing you on the street. You might even meet up with long-lost relatives. The Saints were psyched to visit Canada for MuchMusic's Snow Job in B.C. this spring. "I can't wait to go back there," Nat said. "I Know Where It's At" is already on Canada's Top 10. "I heard from family members I've never met before. It's wild."

The downside: Queer cuisine native to the country you're visiting (Toto, I've a feeling we're not in Kansas anymore!). So . . . where does one get a spot of tea and crumpets in the Big Apple? Then there's the lingo you never studied in school (So what does *sayonara* mean?). Outrageous publicity stunts aimed at getting you noticed (e.g., belting out your new single in the pouring rain in front of an HMV). Endless airports and customs delays—your passport could use some extra pages.

Pencil Me On . . .

The schedule is seriously psycho. Every minute an interview to do, an appearance to make, a plane to catch. Typically it's the band manager's job to be sure that the group members make the most of their visits. If that means not a second to catch their breath, so be it. Hey, that's the price of promoting—since you can't be in two places at the same time (although you try!), you often do phoners (quickie interviews over the telephone, usually from a hotel room).

So, is being a singing sensation glamorous? Sure—if your idea of glamor is scarfing down a slice of cold pizza for dinner while you flip through the cable channels. Or if you enjoy living out of a suitcase and rising at the crack of dawn to be on the set of a morning show at 6 A.M.

Mel: "It's great that we've got a name now—don't get me wrong—but it's work."

The upside: You become gifted at dressing in day-to-evening ensembles that don't wrinkle after 48 hours of wear. And while it's not always fun talking about yourself in interview after interview, there are some surprising moments of self-revelation.

The downside: No time to work out, write a postcard, see the Statue of Liberty.

Nic: "Sometimes we get so busy," she told *Rolling Stone Online*, "I don't have time to pee."

Freeze-Frame

Unless you've been living on Mars, you've seen the Saints' album cover everywhere. Blown up larger than life, the girls grace billboards, subways, and record-store windows, looking positively luscious.

But getting these sexy snapshots is *not* a snap. It takes hours of primping, propping, and posing to achieve perfection in a studio.

Photographer Sean Ellis and a great team of stylists and assistants helped the girls capture their heavenly faces on film—here's how it happens:

A photo studio—usually a big lofty hideaway with high ceilings and huge windows (lots of natural light)—is where the action took place in the Saints' case. While some artists might opt for the outdoors (think of the Beatles strolling across Abbey Road), or pick a posh interior (think Celine Dion sprawled on a velvet antique chair), the Saints chose a white backdrop (called a "seamless") which could be lit with different colored lights (called "gels") to produce different and dramatic effects. A big spotlight makes a halo behind the Saints' heads on the cover (it was no accident!), while inside each girl goes solo in a sultry, blue shadow.

The photographer and his assistants (usually two or three on a shoot) survey the scene, testing the light with a meter, popping flashes, and using a Polaroid camera to get an idea of how the shot will look. The photographer has a lot to think about before he even clicks one frame: Will the photo be soft and shadowy? Will it be sharp and bright? What will we see in the background? Will the shots be posed or impromptu?

Of course the Saints have a lot to say: they want the cover to reflect who they are, not to mention to entice people to buy their album! It was Shaz's idea for her and Mel to show off their tattoos, and the girls all agreed the pic should look relaxed—like they were loungin' around, enjoying their success! They decided a sultry stare would be more appealing than killer-watt smiles. Says Nic, "We like to say things with our eyes!"

The Saints arrived extra early to try on outfits and get their hair and makeup done— this prep time can take as long as four hours (especially with four very headstrong divas directing the show!).

Stylists bring clothing racks loaded with sexy little tank tops to choose from (notice you never see the girls below the waist in these shots? Betcha Shaz has on some baggy old carpenter pants under that baaaad champagne-colored halter!). Black is a popular pick—both Mel and Nick grab dark shoulder-baring tops, while Nat chooses electric blue to emphasize her blue eyes.

Next comes the beauty routine: can you say, mega spray? Not a hair can be out of place in these pics! The girls choose a uniform style—slicked and blown straight—and let their mane makers create magic.

Makeup is also a team theme: glowing skin (that angelic look!), sculpted cheekbones, bold brows, and smoky shadow. Only Nat marches to her own beat: she shuns the au naturel glossy lip color of her bandmates for a sizzling crimson.

When the Saints are all decked out and looking delectable, the photographer calls them over to the set. This guy has to be not only a talented artist, but a great coach as well. It's a little awkward standing up there, twisting and turning, puckering and pouting, while everyone scrutinizes your moves! He talks to the girls, telling them what shots are smokin' and which positions to pass on. The music gets cranked up so the girls will relax and enjoy themselves (a little "Never Ever" blows those nervous butterflies away).

Several rolls of film later, they change outfits, get a quick touch-up, and fly back into frame for another series. In a few hours, it's all over, but the results will be captured forever on their debut album cover. "It's hard work being a supermodel!" laughs Mel. And that ain't no lie!

Get Gorgeous!

Okay, you're posing for your yearbook photo and you gotta be glam—this pic, after all, will be around for all eternity! Some tips from the Saints' session to help you look your best:

1. Rehearse smiling in front of a mirror until you've got it down—which looks better, a back-to-the-last-molar beam or a shy pursed pout? Practice makes perfect!

2. Don't be daring with a new do or makeup color. Now is not the time to try out that fuschia eyeshadow or perm your stick-straight tresses. Either do a test run the month before (it'll grow!) or wait till after the date.

3. Play down the accessories—why detract from your fab face? Those hoop earrings that could double as bracelets—bag 'em. Less is more—make that your law. Notice the Saints are sans jewelry?

4. Follow Nat's example (blue to match her baby blues!)—choose a color that will spotlight your coloring. Yeah, black is a basic—but red revs, cinnamon spices, and jade jazzes.

5. Keep the neckline simple. Cowl and turtlenecks or (heaven help us!) bows bomb in headshots. Your best bet? A crew, V, or buttoned collar. And a word to the wise: save the skin shots for your first CD cover. Pass on the plunge!

Live and On-Person!

So your image is everywhere. Your video plays round the clock on MTV and your single is climbing the charts. Your fans are legion, and they want to see you in action. Time to announce the concert tour! All Saints have said they'll reveal theirs this summer— get your calendars ready, they'll be coming to a stage near you in '98!

Pick a Place . . . But Not Just Any Place

Choosing the theaters, clubs, and stadiums you'll perform in isn't easy. How many seats does it have? Is the stage big enough to boogie on? Is the area easily accessible so that fans will flock from far and wide? How will tickets be sold—through an outlet? At the box office? Details, details. . . . It is said that these girls take an active role in their business. They want to give their fans the best. No doubt they have their hand in these decisions, too.

Hire Some Help

Besides the backup band, performers rely on an army of people to get their show on the road. There's a tour manager (and usually several assistants) who takes care of all the bookings: hotels, food, transport, and so on. Costumers, hair and makeup artists, and choreographers ensure that the singers look supa. Techies carry the mondo equipment—

lights, sets, and speakers—from stage to stage, while lighting and sound experts do their thang behind the scenes. A publicist plans the exposure the band will get in each city (oh no! not another interview!) and makes sure that reviewers are front-row center.

Getting Ready to Rap

The band usually rehearses for a few months before the first concert, working out intricate harmonies and dance moves. They try on countless clothes (that's the fun part!) to find a look that fans will favor—preferably one that will look fly, even if you're watching them from the nosebleed section—and one that can stand up to the workout the girls get onstage.

All Saints Souvenirs

Tour T-shirts, baseball hats, posters, and programs are commissioned. Each item has to be designed, approved by the band and its organizers, and manufactured en masse.

The Big Night

This is the moment you've been working toward all these months—the opening night of your concert tour. You're revved and ready to take on the world! The lights dim, the fans cheer, and you step out onto the stage. You forget the cold pizzas, the crowded hotel rooms, and all those hours traveling. You're a concert queen—and your life will never, ever be the same again. . . .

Chapter 11
The Style File

"*W*e don't dress oversexy," says Saint Nic. "We have a definite look: We wear tanks, hooded sweats, painter's pants, hiking boots, and lots of snowboard gear that we get in Japan. You won't catch us in tiny skirts—we hate being uncomfortable and cold. People are always asking us why we're still in our rehearsal clothes . . . and that's cool."

But style isn't just what you wear. It's the walk. The talk. The 'tude you exude. Ready for a crash course? Get out your notebooks, ladies and gents—we could all learn something from these queens of cool.

General: Street smart and sexy; think gansta rap meets glamor girl; homegirl meets Frederick's of Hollywood. You may raise eyebrows, but they'll never ever forget you!

All Saints Wardrobe 101

Labels to look for: Adidas; Fila; D&G; Tommy; DKNY; Calvin Klein; army/navy surplus.

Boots: Big, black or brown, and ready for battle (Caterpillars, Docs, or Timberland).

Sneakers: Adidas (white or black).

Pants: Baggy, slung low on the hips (to flash a hint of awesome abs); combat trousers or carpenter pants with deep pockets (only you know what hides inside them); drawstring sweats; button-fly jeans in overdyed denim; army fatigues.

Shirts: Tiny tight tanks; sexy sleeveless satins or spandex; mesh football jerseys; cropped white Ts (shop in the little boys' department of your fave store—will it fit a nine-year-old? Perfect!); anything with Japanese writing on it—sooo multiculturally cool!

Jackets: Adidas tracksuits (dig that white stripe); Fila quilted coat (the bigger the better); hooded sweatshirts.

Jewelry: Rings—silver, several and stacked; necklace—a cross on a long Y-chain or thick gold links with matching hoop earrings; a men's sports watch in stainless steel.

Sunglasses: Wraparound shades à la *The Terminator*; lenses look hot in yellow, red, or blue, not just your basic black.

Head gear: Kangol caps; Tommy Hilfiger woolly ski hats; hair clips here, there, and everywhere; cell phone (supercool minuscule) always attached to one ear.

Unmentionables: Wonderbras work magic; little lacey camisoles (to peek out under tanks); men's undershirts, La Senza and Knickerbox undies.

Shopping tips: "I spend my money at the counter with the best-looking men behind it," says Nat.

"Don't be fooled into waiting for sales," adds Shaz. "If you see something you like, buy it anyway."

Beauty Bootie

Hair: "When I don't wash it—and sometimes you just don't have the time—I hide it under a hat," Mel fesses up. Black roots; cinnamon streaks (à la Shaz); slicked into stringy strands with gel (a little dab'll do ya!) or piled high in corn-rowed pigtails. When in doubt, just shake it out. Hair extensions? "Don't knock 'em till ya try 'em," says Shaz.

Lip trick: Red hot . . . or not. The girls go for either sexy, shiny crimson or barely there nudes. Either way, gloss away! Matte's not where it's at. The ladies especially like Mac lipstick and foundation.

Drawing the line: Go heavy on the black or gray liner (think Cleopatra) and smoky shadow. Looking a little like a raccoon? You're ready to sing a Saints tune! Brows are always arched, always dark (no matter what your natural hair color may be). Remember, according to the Saints style, a drama queen steals the scene: best to invest in shadow shades that pack a punch. Two more words of advice: eyelash curlers!

The posse posture: Watch the Saints slink

across the screen in their "Never Ever" video and master their M.O. Hang it loose, hang it low—shoulders hunched, head bowed. Now shuffle. Wanna seem fly? Never look 'em in the eye ... till you're ready for some reckoning.

Saints speak: Say what's on your mind, all the time. Saints never mince words or are afraid to be heard. Unless you're a master of mimicry, you won't be able to do the Brit accent. So settle instead for blending some London lingo into your everyday conversations ("I've got a bloody Bio midterm tomorrow!" "What's on the telly tonight?"). But don't overdo the Mary Poppins bit ("Pip-pip! Cheerio old chap!")—your friends will think you're wack.

Fan Fare: A Portrait of the All Saints Afficionado

Who: Any age, race, sex, nationality—the Saints cross all boundaries (literally and figuratively!) and bridge the generation gap.

If you're an aspiring chanteuse: you wanna BE them.

If you're a fan extraordinaire: You wanna be DOWN WITH them.

Your taste: Anything hot, hip, or happening catches your eye. You're the first in your class to try the new trend—even if it seems a little over the top. You're comfortable with who you are and your clothes communicate this: sometimes they're easygoing (loose and baggy); other times they're sexy and sultry. People might accuse you of being a bit avant garde, but you don't mind. Originality is your middle name and you'd rather be different than wear a guise or compromise your principles.

Musical must-haves: Anything with a beat that gets you on your feet: alternative, techno, hip-hop, rap, and R&B. Hanson is history; you prefer harder, edgier tunes with some rock and soul. Of course, there are always the classics: The British Invasion, The Red Hot Chili Peppers, or a little Aretha or Stevie (he works "wonders" when you're bummed).

Your motto: "If it is to be it's up to me." No one will ever catch you sitting on your bum, waiting for a break. If you want something, you go after it, whether it's the job of Student

Council president or that cute guy in Chem class.

Weekend whereabouts: On a dance floor somewhere; hanging with your fave pals at the mall (and scoping out the new fall fashions); catching the latest fright-fest at the drive-in (a double dose of *Scream* and *Scream II*); or in line all morning for All Saints tix—they just announced their world tour and you've gotta be front-row center!

Where you WON'T be on a Friday night: At home, munching Mallomars and baby-sitting your little bro; brooding by the phone, waiting for Mr. or Ms. Right to call; washing your laundry; washing your hair.

Can't get enough of: English accents, red, white, and blue (the Union Jack flag, that is!); fish and chips and Earl Grey tea; the Saints' CD (you've played it so many times, your mom's threatened to hide it).

Can't deal with: Stuffy, stuck-up types who think they're "all that"; tired pop tunes that are overplayed on the radio (time to sink 'em!); people who judge without any info; all work and no play.

What you strive to be: Real, righteous, ready for anything. A voice for many; a friend to all.

Your idea of heaven: A day (or night) with Nic, Nat, Mel, and Shaz, swapping tales and tunes and learning what it is to live like a Saint.

Your idea of hell: Every Saint CD in Sam Goody is sold out—and there's a six-week waiting list!

Your ideal car: Fast, flashy, maybe fire-engine red with a white-stripe detail (kinda like an Adidas jacket), with a killer stereo system (for blasting you-know-who in your hood).

If you had a million bucks: You wouldn't blow it. You'd share it with your friends and your family (hey, they've always been there for you). Your one splurge? A trip to London to see the Saints play Wembley Stadium, and to follow in their divine footsteps.

If you had one wish: You'd probably pick world peace (you're such a Saint!). But next in line would be the chance to dance and croon an original Shaz Lewis tune—as the fifth band member!

Chapter 12
All Saints Info

*T*o be Saints aware, you gotta see what's out there:

Write to the girls c/o
All Saints Worldwide Fan Club
P.O. Box 50, Stanmore
Middlesex HA7 2US
ENGLAND

The club will also keep you up to date on news and tours.

Some raves and reviews to read up on:

Times Newspapers Limited, October 19, 1997: "Real Girl Power" by Anita Chaudhuri

Spin, January 1998: "Extra Spicey" by

Sylvia Patterson

New York Post, January 11, 1998: "All Saints: Just Sugar and Spice" by Ray Rogers

Disney Adventures, February 1998: "Who's the Next Hanson?" by Bob Cannon

Interview, February 1998: "A Who's Who of the Movie and Music Newcomers Insiders Are Betting On"

Billboard, February 7, 1998: "U.K.'s All Saints Aim for Immaculate U.S. Reception" by Paul Sexton

London Sunday Times, February 22, 1998: "Saint Misbehavin'" by Liz Jones

Toronto Sun, February 24, 1998: "New Brit Girl Band to Sweeten the Charts" by Jane Stevenson

Maxim, March 1998: All Saints album review

Vibe, March 1998: All Saints album review by Chiedo Nkwocha

Request, March 1998: "Saints" by Laurie Jamison

Seventeen, March 1998: "Backstage Pass: All Saints" by Susan Kaplow

People, March 16, 1998: All Saints album review

React, March 16–22, 1998: "Heavenly Creatures" by Michael Krugman

Entertainment Weekly, March 27, 1998: "Extra Spicey" by David Hochman

Jump, April 1998: "New Brits on the Block." A fashion story by Marisa Fox

Way-cool Web Sites

http://www.londonrecords.com The label's official site

Unofficial (yet awesome):

http://www.theallsaints.com/

http://members.xoom.com/ All_Saints_Fan_Site/

http://www.geocities.com/Hollywood/ Academy/6504/

http://www.dsuper.net/~maxoft

http://www.wavenet.co.uk/users/coopes

http://www.webrat.com/allsaints/ Claims to have the largest pic collection on the Net

http://www.fortunecity.com/tinpan/agnetha/246/main.html

http://www.geocities.com/Broadway/Stage/7980/

http://website.lineone.net/~tonk/all-saints/

http://www.geocities.com/SunsetStrip/Palladium/6948/index.htm

http://www.geocities.com/Brodd

http://members.aol.com/saintsuk/index.htm

http://members.tripod.com/~allsaintsrulz

http://members.tripod.com/~Blair_M/AllSaintSindex-2.html

International info:

http://www.angelfire.com/ks/AllSaints/

International All Saints pen pals:

http://www.chez.com/iris/all/saints.htm
A site in French

http://ireland.iol.ie/~kasst/allsaints/

http://www.weblink.force9.co.uk/AllSaints/index.html

http://homepages.newnet.co.uk/gary/AS/

Follow their rise up the charts at:

http://www.billboard.com/

http://www.rollingstone.com

Chapter 13
Heavenly
Horoscopes

*W*hat's in the stars for the All Saints? Check out their astrological outlooks:

Shaznay
October 14
Libra

The inside line: A Libra lady loves to play peacemaker—perfect harmony is her heart's desire (maybe that's why she got her start harmonizing background vocals). You can bet Shaz is the one who works out any All Saints scuffs. Tact is her act—she will do anything to avoid a conflict.

The score on amour: The year ahead for Shaz in the L-O-V-E department is promising! There's just one note she has got to hit. While she can say anything in her songs, it's rumored she's so shy that she's afraid to open up to a guy. So here's a hint, girlfriend: any guy who's fly will appreciate honesty. Say what's on your mind. Give it a shot, Shaz!

The best bloke for her: A total babe minus the 'tude: someone who's absolutely clueless that he could be Leonardo DiCaprio's twin.

Destined to be: Branching out. Libras like to try new things—Shaz's 'scope says she'll be doing something with words. Besides making music, maybe she'll start penning her Saintly story for a movie script!

Nicole
December 7
Sagittarius

The inside line: A Sagittarian lady is proud of her uniqueness—if she has a hard time "fitting in" she'll set new standards. The world is filled with too many possibilities! If she's typical of her sign, Nic tends to be a bit of a fantasizer—but that's okay. She has the creativity and energy to make those big dreams come true.

The score on amour: Sagittarians seek freethinkers who won't make them conform. A Romeo who can wing it is her style—worry-warts need not apply.

The best bloke for her: A guy who's willing to take chances! Nic needs someone who'll go bungee jumping on a whim. This dude will never make unreasonable demands—he thinks Nic's perfect exactly the way she is.

Destined to be: Easing up on the hectic pace. Life feels like it's finally falling into place, and the stars say Nic will be looking for some uncharacteristic calm and quiet—maybe a country home by the sea to retreat to when sheís not taking a world tour with the band?

Natalie
May 14
Taurus

The inside line: Tauruses tend to have the patience of a Saint (no pun intended). Nat's likely the one who encouraged the girls to hang in there and have faith in their future. A stubborn streak sometimes causes conflicts, but if she's a typical Taurus, Nat never takes no for an answer!

The score on amour: Tauruses hate to be tied down and dislike it when a relationship becomes too serious before its time. The stars say she should keep it cool with possessive partners this year. (Not to be confused with adoring fans!)

The best bloke for her: Brains—not just brawn—are what win this woman's heart. Likewise a love who's light and airy and likes to keep her guessing.

Destined to be: Maintaining a healthy regime with regular exercise and a high-energy diet will surely help her keep the unbelievable pace she's already set.

Melanie
March 25
Aries

The inside line: Aries thrive on a challenge—just throw an obstacle in their path and they'll charge it! If Mel's a typical ram, she gets revved when something new and unknown appears on her doorstep. Her motto might be: "I'll try anything once."

The score on amour: The stars say someone fascinating—and fiery—is heading her way. Not just someone with a killer bod, but it's a wise and witty gent that the heavens have sent.

The best bloke for her: An Aries lady likes a sparring partner—someone who'll put up a fight and won't fawn over her.

Destined to be: Learning new ways to relax—maybe yoga or meditation. With a hectic schedule looming on the horizon, destressing will be a big priority.

Chapter 14
Test Your
All Saints IQ

1. What spot did "I Know Where It's At" hit on the U.K. charts?

    (a) number one

    (b) number two

    (c) number three

    (d) number four

2. What was the All Saints first big appearance on TV?

    (a) MTV

    (b) VH–1

    (c) The National Lottery Live in Britain

(d) Top of the Pops in Britain

3. What hobby is Nat hooked on?

(a) video games

(b) exercise

(c) needlepoint

(d) coin collecting

4. What is the name of the girl group that often opens for All Saints?

(a) Dynamiss

(b) All Devils

(c) Spice Chicks

(d) Bananarama

5. Which song is *not* on the Saints' album in Japan?

(a) "Alone"

(b) "Beg"

(c) "Trapped"

(d) "Bootie Call"

6. Which song appears on the Saints' album in Japan but *not* in the U.S.?

(a) "Under the Bridge"

(b) "I Remember"

(c) "Take the Key"

(d) "Heaven"

7. Which song features a Steely Dan sampling?

(a) "I Know Where It's At"

(b) "Under the Bridge"

(c) "No More Lies"

(d) "Never Ever"

8. What sporting event theme song did the Saints pass on performing?

(a) Wimbledon

(b) The Winter Olympics

(c) The England World Cup

(d) The U.S. Open

9. What number did the Saints' "I Know Where It's At" single debut at on U.S. charts?

(a) 67

(b) 51

(c) 2

(d) 98

10. Where were the Brit Music Awards
(which All Saints swept!) held?

(a) Madison Square Garden

(b) Wembley Stadium

(c) The Carrier Dome

(d) London Arena

ANSWERS: 1. b; 2. c; 3. b; 4. a; 5. a; 6. b;
7. a; 8. c; 9. b; 10. d.

8–10 correct: You're a Supa Saints Fan. You
know where it's at—and just about
everything about this group. If the girls
ever need a fifth member, they know who
to call.

5–7 correct: You're a Serious Saints Fan.
You could brush up a bit on the band, but
not too shabby. Reread the previous
chapters.

2–4 correct: You're a So-So Saints Fan.

Hello? You need to do some more homework. Your assignment: listen to the All Saints CD every hour until it sinks in.

One or less correct: Saints preserve us! What planet have you been living on? Stop listening to your old Hanson albums and give the girls a go!

Sez Who?

Label which Saint spoke it . . .

1. "Feelings are always starting points for my songs."

2. "I spent most of my childhood tragically out of fashion."

3. "I'd sing for free."

4. "I'm the youngest, so I'm always wearing things that are too big for me."

5. "Dating a celebrity would be a nightmare because the press could totally kill it."

6. "We've always had a bit of an underwear weakness."

7. "I don't even notice when men are

coming on to me."

8. "We're not manufactured—any part of us—we're the real thing."

9. "I've learned a lot just by living."

10. "There are just some people on this planet who have their own motives."

ANSWERS: 1. Shaz; 2. Nic; 3. Mel; 4. Nic; 5. Nic; 6. Nat; 7. Mel; 8. Mel; 9. Shaz; 10. Nat.

Saints Scramble

Can you undo the mixed-up Saints' song titles?

1. YADAMELLMARDA

2. REENVREEV

3. GEREBDRIEDHUNT

4. NEALO

5. DARTPEP

Answers are at the end of the next page.

Heavenly Help

If the girls need a little guidance on a given topic, which Patron Saints should they turn to? Pair 'em with the people they protect:

1. Musicians   (a) Margaret

2. Writers   (b) George

3. Dancers   (c) Francis

4. Businesswomen   (d) Vitus

5. Brits   (e) Cecelia

ANSWERS: 1. e; 2. c; 3. d; 4. a; 5. b

ANSWERS TO SAINTS SCRAMBLE:
1. "Lady Marmalade"; 2. "Never Ever";
3. "Under the Bridge"; 4. "Alone";
5. "Trapped."

Look for These Other Great Titles from HarperActive!

WILL SMITH:

From Fresh Prince to King of Cool
by K. S. Rodriguez

He reigns supreme in television, music, and in the movies, too! Peep out the pages of this book to find out just how Will Smith does it all. His story is the bomb, baby!

THE BACKSTREET BOYS

by K. S. Rodriguez

They're famous, they're hot, and now they're totally yours! Pick up this bio and let the story of the Backstreet Boys drive you wild!

GRAND SLAM STARS:
Martina Hingis and Venus Williams

by Michael Teitelbaum
They played face to face in
the youngest match-up ever
in a Grand Slam final. Now Martina
Hingis and Venus Williams are together
again—in a back-to-back bio!

Way Too Much Information: A Fanatic's Guide to Dawson's Creek

by Sheryl Altman
A bona fide *DC* fanatic offers us a
voyeuristic perspective on the hit TV
show—the girls, the guys, the gossip,
the mind games...everything that makes
Dawson's Creek sizzle. And everything
the ultimate *DC* devotee craves.

A Division of
HarperCollins*Publishers*